MASKS &
CROCODILE

YANG LIAN

MASKS & CROCODILE

A Contemporary Chinese Poet and His Poetry
Translations and Introduction by Mabel Lee
Illustrations by Li Liang

UNIVERSITY OF SYDNEY EAST ASIAN SERIES NUMBER 3

Published by WILD PEONY PTY LTD
PO Box 636 Broadway NSW 2007 Australia

First Published 1990

National Library of Australia
Cataloguing-in-Publication entry
Yang, Lian, 1955-
    Yang Lian masks and crocodile: a contemporary Chinese poet and his poetry.

    ISBN 0 9590735 7 4.

    1. Yang, Lian, 1955- –Criticism and interpretation.
    I. Lee, Mabel. II. University of Sydney. III. Title.
    (Series: University of Sydney East Asian series.)

895.1152

Cover design by Paul Soady

Set in 14½ on 20 point Jenson by Adtype Photocomposition, Sydney on Linotype L300 typesetter.

Printed and bound in Australia by National Capital Printing, Fyshwick, ACT.

CONTENTS

Also published by Wild Peony:

Tanizaki Jun'ichiro, *A Cat Shōzō and Two Women.* Translated by S. Matsui. University of Sydney East Asian Series. *150 pp. ISBN 0 9590735 5 8.*

Shijin: Autobiography of the Poet Kaneko Mitsuharu 1895-1975. Translated by A. R. Davis and edited by A. D. Syrokomla-Stefanowska. University of Sydney East Asian Series. *324 pp. ISBN 0 9590735 3 1.*

Kam Louie, *Between Fact and Fiction: Essays on Post-Mao Chinese Literature and Society. 149 pp. ISBN 0 9590735 6 6.*

Readings in Modern Chinese. Compiled by Liu Wei-ping, Mabel Lee, A. J. Prince, Lily Shaw Lee and R. S. W. Hsu. *161 pp. ISBN 0 9590735 4 X.*

Basic Chinese Grammar and Sentence Patterns. A. D. Syrokomla-Stefanowska and Mabel Lee. *99 pp. ISBN 0 9590735 1 5.*

Putonghua: A Practical Course in Spoken Chinese. Mabel Lee and Zhang Wu-ai. *101 pp. ISBN 0 959735 0 7.*

Available from:
The Canterbury Press Pty Ltd
Unit 2, 71 Rushdale Street
Scoresby Victoria 3179 Australia
Phone (03) 764 2777 Fax (03) 764 2833

BIOGRAPHICAL DETAILS

Yang Lian: Born 22 February 1955, Bern, Switzerland where he lived for one year while his parents were posted in the Chinese Embassy there. He grew up in Beijing and began to publish "modernist" poetry in 1979. He has published in China the three collections *Ritualization of the Soul* (*Li hun;* 1985), *Desolate Soul* (*Huang hun,* 1986) and *Yellow* (*Huang,* 1989). A large number of his poems were published in English translation by John Minford, Séan Golden and Alisa Joyce in *Renditions* (1983 & 1985). Karl-Heinz Pohl has published a selection of Yang Lian's poetry in German, *Pilgerfahrt* (1987).

Mabel Lee: Senior Lecturer in the Department of East Asian Studies of the University of Sydney is co-editor of the *University of Sydney East Asian Series* and assistant editor of the *Journal of the Oriental Society of Australia.* She is co-author of *Putonghua: A Practical Course in Spoken Chinese* (1984; repr. 1989), *Basic Chinese Grammar and Sentence Patterns* (1986; repr. 1989) and *Readings in Modern Chinese* (1987). Her research is concerned with intellectual trends in 20th century China and her writings in this field have been published in Australia, China and Taiwan.

Li Liang: Born 30 June, 1960, Shanghai, China is a graduate in scenic design of the Shanghai Drama Institute. He worked as a set designer with China Central Television 1983-7 in Beijing before migrating to Australia. His paintings have been exhibited at The International Art Gallery, Beijing (1986); the Shanghai Art Gallery (1987); Alvin Gallery, Hong Kong (1987); Le Grand Palais, Paris (1987); The Arts Club, London (1987); Galerie Lang, Vienna (1987) and Artmet, Sydney (1988). His work has been collected by the Art Gallery of New South Wales in Sydney.

THE BOOK OF EXILE

You are not here   Marks of this pen
Just written are swept off by a wild wind
Emptiness like a dead bird soars across your face
Funereal moon is a broken hand
Turning back your days
Back to the page when you do not exist
In writing   You
Bask in your deletion

Like another's voice
Bits of bones are spat carelessly in a corner
Hollow sound of water brushing water
Carelessly enters breathing
Enters a pear and ceases to look at others
Skulls all over the ground are you
In words and lines you grow old in a night
Your poetry invisibly traversing the world

Yang Lian
13th January 1990

THE PHILOSOPHY
OF THE SELF AND YANG LIAN

Yang Lian's association with the poets of the *Today (Jintian)* magazine group –
Gu Cheng, Beidao, Mang Ke, Shu Ting and Jiang He – who came to
prominence during the Beijing Democracy Wall Movement of late 1978 and
early 1979 has led to his classification as a "modernist poet". "Modernist"
was a vague and general term used synonymously with "misty" to describe
the wave of new poetry which signalled the first clear break from the
themes and concerns of the Yan'an formula of socialist-realist literary creation which was prescribed for all endeavours in art and literature, a formula which was rigidly enforced during the Cultural Revolution period.

   In early 1979 soon after Yang Lian rushed from Guangxi province back
to Beijing to take part in the Democracy Wall Movement, he was introduced by Gu Cheng to the *Today* group and began to take part in their
weekly meetings on literature. From August he began to write "modernist"
poems, some of which were published in *Today*: "Childhood" (Tongnian)
was published in No. 6, "Because Of" (Weile) and "Earth – Colour" (Tudi –
yanse) in No. 8 and "We Rise From Our Own Footprints" (Women cong
zijide zuji shang) in No. 9. When the magazine ceased publication in 1980
under pressure from the authorities, the poets re-grouped under the new
name of the Today Literature Research Society (Jintian Wenxue Yanjiu
Hui) and began the publication of *Source Materials of the Today Literature
Research Society (Jintian wenxue yanjiu hui ziliao)*. Yang Lian had two poems published in this magazine: "Song of Blue-coloured Ravings" (Lanse
kuangxiang qu) in No.1 and "Black Canopy Boat" (Wu peng chuan) in No.
3. He was one of the seven elected councillors of the new publication along
with Beidao, Mang Ke, Jiang He, Ling Bing and E Fuming, and edited No.
3 of the new publication which was also to be its last. In the intermittent
bouts of precarious liberalization laced with sudden clampdowns in the
Chinese intellectual world of the 1980s, these poets gradually shifted from
the exhilarating Beijing environment of the late 1970s which had united
them temporarily as a group with the common aim of self-expression in the
poetic medium.

During the 1980s most members of the group have had the opportunity for travel abroad; today many of them are still living abroad. This decade saw vigorous growth in the translation into Chinese of Western literature, literary criticism and philosophy; strong centres of comparative literature studies were also established in China. Access to such writings as well as travel abroad broadened the horizons and perspectives of these poets but while they remain united in soul in their call for freedom of the individual and human rights in China, their creative paths in poetry have become distinctly different. They are no longer the young men and women they were a decade ago living in isolation from the rest of the world as decreed by the Cultural Revolution; their experiences, their gradual growing to maturity in their personal lives, as well as in their commitment to poetry have separated them in distance in their poetry and they can no longer be considered the closely-knit poetry group they once were.

Yang Lian states that he first began to read translations of Western literature in 1978. This was several years later than his fellow poets of the *Today* group. Prior to that time his poetic instincts had found expression in the writing of classical poetry. He recalls that in 1978 he wrote some two hundred classical poems, but swept up in the activities of the "modernist" poetry of the *Today* group, he totally abandoned classical poetry and began to write "modernist" poetry. He assumed that his abandonment of classical poetry was final, for he did not think to keep any of those unpublished poems. However an examination of Yang Lian's creative output as a total entity dating from the late 1970s to the present reveals that his early association with classical poetry probably dictated the direction his poetry was to take and has sustained his continued development as a poet. Despite the modern thematic concerns and imagery, his use of the modern language, and his being sole arbiter of the style and form of his own poetry, one can still clearly detect the "music" of classical poetry which resounds through all of his poetry. Furthermore, a strong sense of communion with poets of the past permeates his poetry, revealing a philosophy of poetry long established as tradition among Chinese poets over the centuries.[1] However Yang

---

1 A. R. Davis makes some important statements on the practice of communication through poetry of Chinese poets of one period with those of previous periods in "Su Shih's 'Following the Rhymes of T'ao Yüan-ming's Poems': A Literary or Psychological Phenomenon?", *Journal of the Oriental Society of Australia*, 1 & 2 (1975), pp. 93-108.

Lian is a writer of the present age who, in the 1980s, has reached maturity as a poet with his major work in four books[2] forming the integrated collection entitled ⊕. This motif created by Yang Lian is pronounced *"yi"* of which the circle representing Nature, Heaven and the Sun is cut through the centre by the Chinese character *"ren"*, Man. The symbol ⊕ is a statement that Man is an integral part of Nature and that Nature does not stand in a controlling position over Man.[3] He has given the motif the pronunciation *"yi"* to affirm that *"yi"*, the hexagrams of the *Book of Changes* (*Yijing*), are symbols depicting Nature as perceived by Man who is the arbiter of how Nature is described. At the same time, the vowel component of the archaic pronunciation for *"shi"*, poetry, is *"yi"*, hence ⊕ also emphasizes the central role of poetry and the poet.

Classical poetry was introduced to Yang Lian in the early years of his life prior to his entering primary school in 1962. His father subjected him to a rigorous training which demanded his rote learning of masterpieces of Chinese poetic creation and his listening to them as their meanings were patiently explained. The Tang Dynasty poet Du Fu (712-770) was one of his father's favourites and Yang Lian still recites poems he learnt in those days. This early training of the ear and the mind's eye has been unconsciously exploited by Yang Lian in his "modernist" poetry which now fills several volumes. His poetry is meticulously crafted in the tradition of the classical poets and the "music" of the ancient poets leads him instinctively to words with tonal qualities and sounds which forcefully generate an emotional impact to his poetic images, notwithstanding their modern concerns and freedom from the restraints of the rigid tonal patterns and lines decreed for classical poetry.

2 The four books each comprising sixteen poems are entitled, *The Untrammelled Man Speaks* (*Zizaizhe shuo;* February-June 1985), *In Symmetry With Death* (*Yu siwang duichen;* January-May 1986), *Living in Seclusion* (*Youju;* February-June 1987) and *The Descent* (*Jianglin jie;* March-July 1988). Some of these books have been published in part or as a whole in journals or collections. The poems of the four books were subsequently polished, and at times slightly reworked, into a final manuscript (1988) for publication as the poetic whole in which it was in 1983 originally conceived. My translations from ⊕ in this introductory essay are based on that manuscript.

3 As part of the movement to send educated youths to learn from the peasants, Yang Lian was sent to Changping county near Beijing 1973-1977. It was during this period that he came to the realization that Man stood sandwiched between Heaven and Earth and that Man was every day subjected to torment because of this.

There is yet another important aspect to Yang Lian's training in classical poetry. As was the destiny of all young Chinese of his generation, he was to receive his education in China during the 1960s and 1970s, the two decades of China's recent history when education meant indoctrination in the ideology of the ruling political party. This indoctrination was enforced by the powerful propaganda machinery of the Cultural Revolution when the value and the worth of the individual was totally denigrated. The fictitious Lei Feng was the personification of the ideal Man who was willing to follow the Party unquestioningly; it was him that the masses were exhorted to emulate. During these two decades all literary creation and endeavour were to be identified with the goals of the Party. It was explicitly stated that the sole purpose of literature was to provide positive reinforcement for the political aims of the ruling party.

While the theoretical consequences of literature produced under such conditions could be competently discussed by literary theorists such as Liu Zaifu[4] in the months when the pendulum swung briefly towards liberalization at particular times in the 1980s, the task for creative writers was considerably more difficult. It was Yang Lian's destiny that in the arid educational milieu of the 1960s his early education in classical poetry should be followed in his senior high school years with further reading in classical poetry: his literature teacher was a Beijing University lecturer in classical literature – a specialist in the poetry of the Wei-Jin period – who at the time had been re-allocated to teach in his high school. In this period Yang Lian read the poetry of the Wei-Jin poets Ji Kang and Ruan Ji. It was perhaps another coincidence that in the late 1970s Yang Lian should choose to monitor lectures at Beijing University on classical poetry and on Lu Xun (1881-1936)[5]. It should be noted that classical poetry, particularly the poetry of the Wei-Jin period and the writings of Lu Xun are intimately linked

4 The castration of human characteristics from literature during the Cultural Revolution was systematically analyzed by Liu Zaifu in a series of essays during the mid-1980s. See Mabel Lee, "Rethinking Literature in the Post-Mao Period: Liu Zaifu on the Subjectivity of Literature", *Journal of the Oriental Society of Australia*, 18 & 19 (1986-7), pp.101-125.

5 Lu Xun, still widely acknowledged as the most important thinker and writer of modern China, first rose to fame for his short stories during the May Fourth period. He is important for introducing Nietzschean philosophy to China in his writings, particularly his prose-poems in the collection *Wild Grass* (*Yecao*, 1924-1927) which is his last important collection of creative writing. Thereafter, his creative writings were limited to poetry in the classical form to which he reverted. See my three articles "From Chuang-tzu to

12

to a conception of life and literature deeply rooted in the philosophy of the absolute freedom of the self. Yang Lian, who became aware of his deep fondness for classical literature even before his teenage years, was to imperceptibly absorb this philosophy of the self. Creative literature was the most refined expression of this philosophy which was an integral part of the *Zhuangzi*, a work generally acknowledged as one of China's finest pieces of literary creation. The creative act is born of an all-pervading solitude. It is then that the untrammelled self transcends spatial and temporal boundaries to find expression. The liberating philosophy of the self transmitted through poetry to Yang Lian was to find reinforcement in the philosophy of Nietzsche which in the 1980s again became the single most important Western influence in the Chinese intellectual world. Statements related to the creative process with clearly Zhuangzean and Nietzchean overtones can be discerned throughout the whole of Yang Lian's poetic output.

There had been a Nietzsche craze in Japan at the turn of the century, precisely at the time when young Chinese students were flocking there in thousands to learn the secrets to the wealth and strength of the Western nations. The traditionalist Wang Guowei (1877-1927) who was the first Chinese to attempt to analyze systematically the philosophies of Kant, Schopenhauer and Nietzsche was, as Marian Galik[6] argues, probably drawn to Nietzsche's thinking in 1904-5 because of its aesthetic appeal. Both the revolutionary Zhang Taiyan (1881-1936) and the young Lu Xun (who was for a time Zhang's student in classical studies in Japan) were attracted to what Nietzsche offered as a basic philosophy for human action – this was the philosophy of the untrammelled self which had counterparts in traditional Daoist thinking. This philosophy of the self was a major element of the Chinese anarchist movement centred in Paris and Tokyo many of whose members were to join the Tongmeng Hui (Chinese Revolutionary Alliance) when it was established in Tokyo in 1905. While the compelling

Nietzsche: On the Individualism of Lu Hsün", *Journal of the Oriental Society of Australia*, 17 (1985), pp. 21-38; "Suicide of the Creative Self: The Case of Lu Hsün", A.R. Davis and A.D. Stefanowska (eds), *Austrina: Essays in Commemoration of the Twenty-fifth Anniversary of the Founding of the Oriental Society of Australia* (Oriental Society of Australia, Sydney, 1982), pp. 140-167; "Solace for the Corpse With Its Heart Gouged Out: Lu Xun's Use of the Poetic Form", *Papers on Far Eastern History*, 26 (1982), pp. 145-174.
6 Marian Galik, "Studies in Modern Chinese Intellectual History: V–Young Wang Guowei (1901-1911)", *Asian and African Studies*, 24 (1989), pp. 50-51.

goal of overthrowing the Manchu Qing government, unified many diverse elements among Chinese thinkers and brought about a temporary abandonment of the cause of the individual, as soon as the new Republic was founded in 1912 the unity disintegrated. Nevertheless news of the fall of the Manchus sent Chinese abroad back in droves to their homeland filled with an euphoric optimism that their hope for a strong and wealthy nation with a just society would emerge. Their despair and disappointment by 1915 fermented into an intellectual and cultural revolution which was later named the May Fourth Movement, honouring the student demonstration in Beijing on 4 May 1919. The overriding philosophy of that movement was decidedly anarchist and promoted those aspects of 20th century Chinese anarchism which emphasized the individual and the self. May Fourth student leaders found all politics abhorrent and Nietzsche's thinking, particularly the ideas expressed in *Thus Spoke Zarathustra* and *The Birth of Tragedy*, captured the imaginations of Chinese youth through the new literature of the period. Lu Xun emerged as the most significant writer of the May Fourth period and his creative writings and conception of literary activity were totally at one with those of Nietzsche and Zhuangzi.[7]

The 4 May 1919 student demonstration to protest against the decision of the Allies to hand over German concessions in Shandong province to Japan at the conclusion of World War I was harshly suppressed by the Chinese authorities and as a result, in the ensuing period, Chinese intellectuals increasingly turned to political activism. As they perceived the threat to the nation increase, their struggle for goals for the individual and the self weakened. Clearly perceiving the tragic consequences of a revolution in the style of the Russian one for the creative writer, Lu Xun whose writings embody the spirit of May Fourth, committed his creative soul to the grave. His prose-poems written in the years 1924-1927 and later published as a collection with the title *Wild Grass* bear testimony to this painful decision.[8] He had thought that to cease writing creatively would leave him like a corpse with its heart gouged out but his creative self was provided solace by

---

7 See my article, "May Fourth: Symbol of Bring-It-Here-Ism For Chinese Intellectuals", *Papers on Far Eastern History*, 48 (forthcoming March 1990).

8 Lu Xun cites the example of the Russian poets Sobol and Yesenin who smashed themselves to death on the epitaph of the revolution which they had so fervently promoted. See "Suicide of the Creative Self: The Case of Lu Hsün", pp. 166-167.

his return to the writing of classical poetry, a form which he had not used since he began his career as a creative writer in the May Fourth period.[9]

In the case of Lu Xun it was a conscious choice to abandon the writing of creative literature as he knew it. For many other writers of a lesser intellect and of less deep a commitment to the concept of literature implicitly expounded in the *Zhuangzi* and *Thus Spoke Zarathustra* it was perhaps not painful to write the socialist-realist literature required of writers. The sacrifice of goals for the self, for so lofty a goal as patriotism, seemed justified. Moreover, if there is no commitment to the concept of literature as extolled by Zhuangzi and Nietzsche, both of which embrace a commitment to the philosophy of the self, then no conscious decision needs to be made at all. Certainly no other writer of the time has documented his or her conscious decision to abandon literature. Many young writers gravitated to the communist cause and tried to write literature as prescribed by the Party; others simply ceased to write creatively and turned to other pursuits but this did not allow them to escape criticism and even persecution during the Cultural Revolution for their writings of the past.

It was only after the straightjacket on literary activities was loosened with the death of Mao Zedong in 1976 and the fall from power of the Gang of Four, that writers and critics began timidly to survey the barren wasteland of Chinese literature since the May Fourth era. The writings of the *Today* poets represent the optimism of youth as did the whole of the Democracy Wall Movement of the late 1970s. The continuing threat of arbitrary government suppression of demands for personal freedom and civil rights was demonstrated by the arrest of Wei Jingsheng, March 1979, which forced the movement underground but succeeded in bringing a halt to public rallies for democracy until April-June 1989. Nevertheless, the 1980s saw a heightening of the demand for freedom of expression particularly in literature and at the same time repeated suppression of such demands, even if such demands were backed by the authority of the early writings of Marx and expressed by dedicated Party writers such as Wang Meng, Liu Zaifu and Liu Binyan.

In 1977 Yang Lian joined the literature unit of Central Broadcasting and was thus able to escape what seemed to him "a death sentence" as

---

9 See "Solace for the Corpse With Its Heart Gouged Out: Lu Xun's Use of the Poetic Form".

a farmworker in Changping county near Beijing where he had been sent for re-education by the peasants. With the financial security of his new position as a professional writer, for the first time he had the opportunity to read widely in both classical Chinese and Western literature, both of which had been proscribed during the Cultural Revolution.

As mentioned earlier, the 1980s was a period when the meaning of literature was re-examined. There was a revived Nietzsche craze amongst Chinese intellectuals and an attempt to link China's present with the May Fourth tradition and its spirit of personal freedom and democracy. It was in this context that Yang Lian like many of his contemporaries read Nietzsche's *Thus Spoke Zarathustra,* noting Nietzsche's message for meaningful existence and in particular for the creative writer. In 1985 Yang Lian wrote the sixteen poems of *The Untrammelled Man Speaks* which evokes a "Zarathustran" feeling both in sound effect and in its Nietzschean message. *The Untrammelled Man Speaks* is the first of the four books of the collection ♀ which he considers to be his most important work. He had begun to conceive the framework of ♀ in 1983: the *Book of Changes* was to be its inner framework but the order was to be re-arranged to emphasize the significance of the "changes" as the Chinese system for symbolizing Nature. The four books of ♀ were conceived as a total entity.

Throughout the early 1980s, as they became available in Chinese translation, Yang Lian avidly read representative works in the poetry, drama, fiction and criticism of Japan, England, Ireland, Germany, Spain, France, Russia, Czechoslovakia, Poland, Romania, Greece, Italy, United States, Mexico, Peru, Argentina, Chile, India and Columbia. However, he states a general preference for "traditional writers" and singles out for special mention Dante whose *Divine Comedy* he equates in greatness with the poetry of Qu Yuan (c. 340 B.C. – c. 278 B.C.). For him, Qu Yuan stands above all other Chinese poets for his independence of thinking. The boldness and the symbolic act of Qu Yuan's "Questions Addressed to Heaven" (Tian wen) with its series of questions he finds even surpasses Dante. Yang Lian maintains that the use of the unanswered question form by Qu Yuan is an expression of poetic genius and in 1983 was himself inspired to write the series of eight poems *Questions Addressed to Heaven.*[10] In the case of more

---

10 Yang Lian, *Yellow* (*Huang*; Renmin Wenxue Chubanshe, Beijing, 1989), pp. 7-17.

16

recent writers, he expresses admiration for Samuel Beckett and W. B. Yeats: Beckett's portrayal of human emotions in *Waiting for Godot* is "excellent" and W. B. Yeats' later works reveal "superb analyses" of human fate. On his completion of the sixteen poems of *In Symmetry With Death,* which constitutes the second book of ⊕, he came to read Ezra Pound's epic poem *Cantos* which he describes as portraying the artist's ideal, the very ideas he had sought to express in *In Symmetry With Death*. His reading of foreign writings dwindled after this as he became totally immersed in writing the remaining two books of ⊕, *Living in Seclusion* and *The Descent,* which were completed in 1987 and 1988 respectively. Fragments of the first three books of ⊕ have appeared in Taiwan and Hong Kong publications; in China, eight of the sixteen poems of *The Untrammelled Man Speaks* and the whole of *In Symmetry With Death* were included in *Selected Poems of Five Writers (Wuren shixuan)*[11]. But ⊕ was conceived as a total entity and should be read as such. As the names of the four books suggest, while ⊕ uses the framework of the *Book of Changes,* the total conception strangely resounds with the journey of Zarathustra and less distinctly with the philosophy of literature of poets such as Tao Yuanming (?376-427) and the Wei-Jin poets who have been labelled by later generations as "Daoist", an indictment of their lack of concern for the problems of society. These early Chinese poets did not theorize on the creative process; they simply created the beautiful poetry for which generations have held them in awe without necessarily comprehending the emotions behind and motivations for their writings. Chinese writers of the 20th century have been drawn to Nietzsche because he defines through Zarathustra the journey of the creative writer. Nietzsche gave a more concrete expression to what they as writers vaguely experienced in their writing of literature. Perhaps it was Lu Xun's philosophy of the self, or what might be called Nietzschean perspective, together with his profound knowledge of Chinese history which allowed him to discern the social implications of the seemingly "escapist" poetry of the past.[12] Yang Lian too has a strong commitment to history; and like Lu Xun, treats the individual self as the basis for the interpretation of history of which the individual is an integral component. Yang Lian perceives Man

---

11 Zuojia Chubanshe, Beijing, 1986, pp. 22-82.
12 See "From Chuang-tzu to Nietzsche: On the Individualism of Lu Hsün".

not only as a part of China, but as a part of the history of mankind. He has consciously sought to acquire a knowledge of the past and to reflect on it. For Yang Lian, Lu Xun is a part of Chinese history. Significantly, the sixteen poems of *The Descent* which constitutes the final book of ℗, portrays the return of Yang Lian the poet to the concerns of his immediate environment.

Apart from ℗, in the early 1980s Yang Lian also completed a number of smaller collections which encompass specific areas of his intellectual and poetic development. The collection of prose-poems *Child by the Sea* (*Haibian de haizi*, 1982)[13] concludes an early phase of reflection on his personal history and sings with ecstasy of his discovery that poetry is within himself and his realization of the significance of poetry to his own life and to the life of mankind. Throughout the collection there are repeated affirmations of the decision to commit himself to poetry. The poems are also infused with an identifiably Nietzsche-Zarathustra and Lu Xun-*Wild Grass* texture, which one might also describe as Kafkaesque, and with his generation's youthful optimism for love and hope in the midst of a harsh Chinese reality: "Life is a forest surging defiantly out of filthy soil and flowing in a raging torrent towards the sea." ("Blessings" No. 3) He discovers that the self is a part of the cosmos and he jealously guards this self: "The sun blazes and the stars shine, showing me every instant that I am a part of the cosmos, a world, a dream. No-one can steal my heart's self." ("Blessings" No. 7) However he acknowledges that with his new awareness, life is to be a tortuous, eternal personal quest as shown below in "Blessings" No. 8 which is strikingly reminiscent of Lu Xun's *Wild Grass* collection.

The fact that Yang Lian, at the time of writing *Child by the Sea*, had only read a few of the *Wild Grass* poems is interesting and reveals an inherent affinity with Lu Xun in both philosophical concerns and poetic imagery. The distinctly Zarathustran feeling conveyed in *Wild Grass* confirms Lu Xun's commitment to Nietzsche's message for the creative writer[14] as do the poems of *Child by the Sea* confirm Yang Lian's. Interesting too is the fact that the prose-poem form employed in these collections by Lu Xun and Yang Lian is close to the style employed by Nietzsche in *Thus Spoke*

---

13 This largely unpublished collection comprises four books, each containing fifteen poems: *Blessings* (*Zhufu*); *Wandering* (*Manyou*); *Praise* (*Zanmei*) and *Dedication* (*Fengxian*).
14 See "From Chuang-tzu to Nietzsche: On the Individualism of Lu Hsün".

Zarathustra: the similarity of the concerns of these three poets and the result-ing images they were compelled by some inner force to express in poetry have led to a similar feeling in these works. Only a small handful of the poems of *Child by the Sea* have found their way into publications but even as early as 1982 when the collection was completed some of the themes and images which were later to be given different forms of poetic treatment in ♀ and in *Masks and Crocodile* were already beginning to emerge. The follow-ing poems from *Child by the Sea* constitute fragments of Yang Lian's own history of his "self".

You say: "Don't worry! Hurry along – " You will appear at a certain point along this road although you do not actually tell me where.
I can only search for you each dark night at the end of the road.
The sound of tapping, like raindrops splashing the grey sky, each second wounds my heart. To greet you, my small room burns all night with a solitary lamp.
Treetops in the unfathomable depths of the night make a deafening noise, like terror from the depths of the soul. Is it you? Strange cursing pours into my thinking like a waterfall.
Hasn't the time come yet? Can't the end of the road be seen yet? I hate my own foolishness, my hope and my despair. But my eyes still untiringly turn to the end of the road.
I pray: My boat voyages in the eternal darkness. Heading towards that unknown destination, in the instant when finally the road and the dawn merges – inside my heart, there are only blessings.

"Blessings" No. 8, *Blessings*

For Yang Lian, the individual holds mankind's history within himself and he defines what he sees as his chosen calling as a poet. At the same time, he begins to speak of the sea as his "old village", i.e. the place where he was born. His close association with the sea is established in *Child by the Sea* as a symbol of eternal Nature of which all mankind is a part.

The path we tread keeps stretching dismally further, so what hope are we given?
The path that we tread slowly compresses the colours of rock fragments into the history of each person.

"Blessings" No. 9 (extract), *Blessings*

Let the lusting heart of the poet for ever be shamed by the magnificence of Nature!
Like a child, everywhere – I shall learn to bring blessings to the remote corners
of the wilderness.

"Blessings" No. 12 (extract), Blessings

Looking with the eyes of a child, the world becomes as pure as myself. Discarding
everything I shall go forth, to fuse life with this ever-rippling music.
I have long belonged to you – oh songs of my old village. Before becoming a mysterious seed I was the wind drifting everywhere in the wilds. A carefree wanderer,
no-one is more familiar than me with your ancient tales.
Looking with the eyes of a child, the world becomes as pure as myself. My laughter
gleams like a sickle just sharpened, is infused with the brittleness and scent of
dried-out bundles of hay.
I have long belonged to you – oh earth of my old village. That first parting to this
day still saddens me. Each day I sit by the riverside, dreaming that I shall return
to your bosom singing with the flowing water: I shall forget the lies, the
loneliness and the hatred, and through dying regain joyfulness!

"Blessing No. 14", Blessings

All endings are not endings, all beginnings are not beginnings.
I should leave, the sea is calling me. Like the leaf silently drifting down to welcome
the early autumn, I am beginning the only wandering of a life which is my
own.
There is no farewell. Words of good wishes too have been carried away on the wind.
There is no refuge. The winding path of the soul cuts through the world and time,
that expanse of bustling wilderness. The heavy scent of wild reeds weaves an
endless night for dreaming.
The dark corner where as a child I wept for a long time cannot detain me, nor can
my loved one linking my arms in a lovers' knot.
I am beginning the only wandering of a life which is my own, although even now I
do not know what awaits me – the ripples which mysteriously agitated my
thinking as a child – wherein lies the source of their eternal energy?

"Wandering" (extract), Wandering

In a world of unseeing people, Yang Lian affirms his belief in the self and indicts the unseeing world of which he realizes he is a part, yet from which he is alienated:

I seek nothing of you, I seek only light!
I weep of nothing to you, I seek only light!
The poet says: I came to this world to see the sun. But why have I wandered into this
world, surely not just to hear the sound of a bamboo cane tapping on the
ground, stabbing a heart of darkness?!
I roam through countless streets and lanes, the road ahead is for ever bumpy.
I grope around in a stream of festival-goers, like a discordant note.
I have heard much ridicule and my body bears the scars of naughty children's tor-
ments. But what can I say to them? – My tears were all swallowed in that
corner which I called home.
There is no morning, no dusk. Spring comes with the twittering of sparrows. I reach
out to hold up the sun but am blocked by a shadow which drifts in from
somewhere. People say it is a cloud –
A cloud is something of beauty but this brings me only indifference and dis-
illusionment....
My breathing is blind, my blood is blind. I have passed through many places but
nowhere in my memory are there any images.
My body is the boundary which my soul cannot transcend. I am alive, like an
innocent prisoner. At birth my eyes were wrapped in a black cloth and all this
time I have been imprisoned in my own night – like that of all humanity, my
heart turns to light, enduring a sadness more terrible than death, a wasteland
stripped of love.

....

I know: My shouting is blind, my imagination is blind. As my voice disperses into
the air, I am like a child staring hopelessly at the kite in the distance. But I am
still a blind person, an innocent convict, bearing a fate which I cannot remove,
imprisoned in the night of the years and the months – with a heart of darkness
and eyes with no light I see all of this.
Yes, blind people, curse this world without light, this world where even convictions
are blind, where even people's goals are blind – passing through the clamour of
dawn, all those eyes open with the sun, I feel a sense of elation: It is no-one but
myself, staring hard at the shadows which suffocate our lives....
I roam through countless streets and lanes, the road ahead is for ever bumpy.
I grope around among streams of festival-goers, like a discordant note.
But I am growing, I know that I am growing, and moreover like the myriad things

of Nature, through some mystical formula my own light begins to emanate. Perhaps, it is only in the way of the poet that the blind can – procure light.

"Blind People" (extract), *Wandering*

The theme of the blindness which imprisons the individual from birth is developed and expanded in the other poems of *Child by the Sea* and becomes the fundamental construct of his criticism of man in society around which all of his poetry is built. The vibrant symbol of the sea, which is frequently used in his poetry, is also established in this collection as the source of raw passion, energy and life: "The sea created you and also is set afire because of the light you create, generating the trembling and radiant ecstasy of an unruly young woman when she is for the first time possessed." ("About the Sun", *Wandering*) The image of death and the grave which figure prominently throughout all of Yang Lian's later poetry is also established in *Wandering*:

This is a dream, a parable. This is my own epitaph.
........................:........................
The land of my dreams is covered with rocks and graves. I am running, my feeble
    footsteps sinking deeper into the mire. I call out to the moon, but my lips are
    locked in deathly silence. There is only terror and swaying, smoky green
    shadows drenching the years and the months. Disguised springtimes pour
    thickly into a deep abyss which cannot be transcended....
This is a dream. This is destiny. This is a story more true than memory.
I don't know when it started, I lost myself – lost love, that wild passionate drop of
    blood flowing from my ancestors; lost freedom, the countless roads stretching
    in all directions to embrace the sun; lost youth, a youth chaste and naked like
    jasmine, so insatiable that all hopes were committed to a small pair of fragrant
    hands. But where is all this now? I have even lost hatred, that chaste torch
    which seems to roar jubilantly alongside dark night, to hold high a dawn
    ripped into fragments.
I weep in a prison of my own making. Perpetually alienated from others, and even
    perpetually alienated from myself: an aged and painful life, riddled with
    wounds, is secretly imprisoned behind inexplicable smiles. That joyfulness, like
    the bright red and green painted onto children's faces, tortures the unsleeping
    heart which has not yet been painted, weaving each night's secrets....

"Self" (extract), *Wandering*

While Yang Lian can be seen to have strong philosophical links with Lu Xun and the Nietzschean tradition in creative literature, there is a distinct difference in historical time between the two writers. Yang Lian consciously acknowledges history. He is fully aware that his history embraces that of Lu Xun's times and that of the times since then. Further, unlike Lu Xun who consciously resolved that his instinct and talent for literary creation should suicide, Yang Lian is very single-mindedly pursuing a total commitment to poetic creation. The essential meaning of poetry, the conscious manipulation of words to serve the poet are themes interwoven into his poetry. More than any other Chinese poet of modern times, his poetry may be considered poetry about poetry, this may certainly be said to be a feature of *Masks and Crocodile*. For Yang Lian, the May Fourth innovations in literature followed a negative approach in seeking to change the language to suit the ideas writers wanted to convey. His approach is positive: he firmly believes that language can be made to serve the writer and it is this which he seeks to achieve in his poetry. A sense of history, the innovative use of language, the extension of knowledge into the past as well as spatially outwards and the function of solitude for reflection on newly acquired knowledge are prerequisites for the conscious act of poetry for Yang Lian and places him in a unique position in the history of modern Chinese poetry.

> The tears of language, convulsively gush forth with the soul's wounds, forging them into gifts for the world. But these volumes of heroic historical epic are eventually also discarded by the children, and like the years and the months grow withered and yellow, like the echoes of the wind sink into an emptiness of eternal oblivion –
> "What is the purpose of it all?"
>
> "Praise" No. 5 (extract), *Praise*

> I wonder who that child is?
> The child with a blue handkerchief pinned to his chest, his eyes so blue as if the whole of life's mysteries had been written into them. His face is a beautiful dream.
> The child on the soft sand, just learning to walk, prattling as if talking with the waves – has come alone to the seashore of the world.
> I wonder who that child is?

The sun and the sea have saturated him, he radiates light – his heart is like a shining
   nest of woven sunlight and contains mysterious songs. Laughing, he smashes
   through the boundaries between the world and himself, cutting across the
   tangled flight of the centuries.

Yes, the sparse footprints he leaves on the sand, uses the sea's timeless inscription for
   memory's epitaph. The profound riddle, sacred like a tear of joy suspended in
   heaven.

He is too small, too small to even remember his mother's face and certainly unable to
   guess at his future. He can only move towards it blindly and enquiringly, without turning back –

What if there is a tempest in the distance?

The world is still something for children to laugh about!

I wonder who that child is?....

"Dedication" No. 15, *Dedication*

Yang Lian travelled to the Chinese hinterland: Guangxi in 1978,
Shaanxi, Sichuan and Hubei in 1980-1981, Gansu in late 1981 and Qinghai
and Xizang (Tibet) in 1983. He perceived travel in the Chinese hinterland as
a means to increasing his understanding of the history of the vast land of
which he was an integral part. His childhood home in Beijing, after his
parents returned with him as an infant from Switzerland (where Yang Lian
was born), was situated close to the ruins of the Yuanming Yuan and the
back section of Yihe Yuan which had fallen into ruins. The desolate stone
ruins implanted in his mind from early childhood the stark image of
"corpses with arms outstretched to the sky". That he was a part of that
history found confirmation in his observations on man and society in the
Chinese hinterland. At the same time his observations continued to
reinforce his conviction that man in China continued to tread in his own
footprints, seemingly not advancing a step further than his predecessors. It
was as if man had no memory, no history. Yang Lian is acutely aware of the
ghosts of past history which he sees as his own history. "So many forgotten
faces had once lived but now, through the folk art tradition of carving
masks for warding off evil spirits, have shrivelled into a single shadow.
Unmoving laughter; brightly painted-on weeping."[15]

---

15 Yang Lian, "Masks Which Can't Be Taken Off" (Zhaibudiao de mianju); preface to
Masks and Crocodile.

Travel to the hinterland and to the sources of Chinese civilization resulted in the incorporation of new and increasingly stark images into his poetic world. Contact with the vestiges of primitive civilization, also had a liberating effect, and leads his investigation of the self to man's primitive instincts and his physical body. His poetry begins to reveal signs of the maturity which is evident in ♀. In May 1983 *Shanghai Literature* (*Shanghai wenxue*) published the series of five poems entitled *Norlang*, the name of a Tibetan male deity. By July this collection had become the focus of attack in the "anti spiritual pollution" campaign.[16] The campaign proceeded to intensify and during the whole of 1984, he was not to see a single of his poems published. However in 1985 *Norlang* was published in the slim volume *Ritualization of the Spirit* (*Li hun; Young Chinese Poets Series, Shaanxi*, 1985).[17] "Tree of Gold" (Huangjin de shu), the second poem of *Norlang* indicates the sense of liberation he has acquired and vibrates with a primitive virility which he believes is lost in so-called "modern" human society through the gradual denial of Nature.

I am god of the waterfall, god of the snowclad mountains
Tall, strong, lord of the new moon
General of all rivers
Birds roost in my bosom
Dense forests conceal the small path to the secret pond
My unfettered instincts are like a herd of young bucks

Lust like the Third Month
Amassing the force of a tumult

I am a tree of gold
Reaping golden trees
Passionate sensations spring from a deep abyss
Ignoring warnings of the timid all about
Until my waves fill it

Woman wanderer, woman sparkling on the water's surface
Which woman is the only woman forcing me to drink

---

16 See for example Lu Yang's analysis of the poem series *Norlang*: "Don't Mistake Decadence for Something Wonderful" (Mo ba fuxiu dang shenqi), *Shikan*, 1 (1984).
17 All the poems of *Norlang* have recently been republished in *Yellow*, pp. 100-106.

My eyes conquer the night
Twelve trumpets conquer the guava-flower wind
Wherever I go, there are no shadows
Every strawberry I touch transforms into a brilliant star rising in the centre of the
world
Possessing all of you, I, the true male

"Tree of Gold", Norlang

In February 1985, Yang Lian began the writing of ⊕/K which he acknowledges as his "most important work". Two years earlier, in 1983, he had mentally started to design the framework for this work. The *Book of Changes* is used as its inner structure, but he pulls it apart and re-arranges the sequence to emphasize the significance of this ancient classic as the Chinese system for symbolizing Nature. The underlying message of ⊕/K is that the centuries of interpretations given to the *Book of Changes* had become totally divorced from its original and basic intent. The sixty-four hexagrams are symbolic representations of Nature *as perceived* by Man, they do not represent the elements controlling Man. Man is the agent observing Nature of which he himself is an integral part. However, over the ages man has atrophied within himself, a process beginning at birth; he exists as a living corpse. His face is but a mask enclosing the ugly stench of decaying flesh wriggling with maggots. This symbol of the corpse extends to embrace the whole of Chinese society, strangled by institutions which have usurped Man's authority as arbiter of the actions, thinking and emotions of the self.

It is in the four years during which ⊕/K was written that we see Yang Lian achieve maturity as a poet. The descriptions of raw primitive passion and youthful virility of the *Norlang* poems completely disappear and there emerge the powerful, black, haunting and grotesque images which have become permanent features of his poetry. Many of the actual images from ⊕/K resurface later in *Masks and Crocodile*. By June 1985 he had completed the sixteen poems of *The Untrammelled Man Speaks* and thereafter travelled for three months on the high loess plains of Shaanxi. The second book, *In Symmetry With Death,* was written during January-March of 1986; in May-August he travelled to Hong Kong, West Germany, France, Spain, England and Austria where he gave poetry readings and lectures. At the beginning of 1987 he wrote fifteen short poems with the title *Scenery in a*

Room (*Fangjianli de fengjing*)[18], then during February-June completed the third book of ◉, *Living in Seclusion*, travelling to Guizhou in July. From August to October he completed a volume *Man's Self-Awakening* (*Ren de zijue*) in which he examines the problems experienced in contemporary Chinese culture and investigates their connections with traditional cultural traditions. In this work, Yang Lian uses the prose form to expand and clarify themes which already exist in his poetry. The final book of ◉, *The Descent* was written March-July 1988 and on 3 August he left Beijing for Australia for a six-month visit to take part in the Spoleto Arts Festival in Melbourne and the Carnivale Festival in Sydney.

During Yang Lian's stay in Australia he wrote two series of thirty poems, *Masks* and *Crocodile,* which are published together as a single collection in this volume as *Masks and Crocodile.* I have translated a selection of poems from each of the four books of ◉ to serve as a backdrop for reading *Masks and Crocodile* which is an extraction of ideas developed in ◉, but using a completely different poetic format: that of highly compressed short lines arranged into six-line poems. The poems collected in ◉ are complex in thought and in artistic arrangement and furthermore embody many layers of meaning. It is hoped that this small selection from ◉ will provide readers with a taste of the poetic dimension and strength of style of Yang Lian's major work, much of which remains unpublished, either in the original Chinese or in translation. I have based these translations on the final unpublished version of ◉ which was finalized for publication in 1988.

Throne: Spilling forth from light, honouring only the invasion of this land
Throne: Spilling forth from clear-sounding bronzes, startling words inherited by the
    prophet
From nowhere as far as the eye can see, mountains like an altar
         The day the mouth opens
         Smoke of wolf dung curls up[19]
         From floral sleeves, vast expanses of disease splashing into a starry
            pattern
    Language of the dead, invading my lips not inoculated against rotting
    A vegetable of fat flesh
    Sprouts forth hedonistic grasses, drinking like the new moon

18 *Yellow,* pp. 23-45
19 In ancient China, wolf dung was burnt at border posts to give the signal for alarm.

Surge of feverish trembling, only excuse for sleeping in the open on
eternally dark nights
Blushing from eulogies, the fashionable lies
Throne: Spilling forth from the sealed silence of bone joints
The more feeble world cowers to quietly listen
In an instant, a deathly voice
I am the prophet I do not know, I am my own testament
I speak the words carried into the epitaph of the I who has died
Inducing a drop of semen
I am spat out by another, to disseminate a pure progeny in this land of the dead
Many go to the mountain ranges, rotting corpses in the same cold
palace
Many obituaries in the shape of sleeping beauties
Empty valleys, between the legs there is burning, wanton bushes
appear and disappear in ashes
Endless reverberations
In intervals of my singing, birds in flocks soar high
Trees of jade green, mountains deep like a pond of quiet water
Butterflies spill forth, sleepwalking from lotus to lotus
Heart speaking irrepressibly, like a light impulsively shining
From dead-end roads gradually rising
From ears full of suffering, awakening prehistoric monsters of Black
Death
Lust for dried bones invading curses
I conquer my kingly glory
I go far from myself, continually renewing, removing wind and dust like taking
off a gold-plated mask
Pass through death in words to squander non-death –
Pedigree of ghosts propagated by a chisel
Decree-promulgating Heaven grows and deepens until totally naked,
swallowing and spitting out the source of the Universe

"Heaven" No. 3, *The Untrammelled Man Speaks*

In the second book of $\frac{\oplus}{\wp}$, *In Symmetry With Death,* Yang Lian confronts
his audience with the historical past. Through the use of historical figures
and legends as masks or symbols, he constructs a totally new poetic
language and imagery which links present man with the past. The sixteen
poems each given a classification of "earth" or "mountain" are arranged

symmetrically. The following three poems from *In Symmetry with Death* provide some indication of the widening scope of his thinking and his development as a highly experimental poet, both in language and poetic form.

"Now, lust is death"
>   Have you gone mad? The setting sun in the afternoon is still far away throbbing out a vast turmoil
Gold colours profound and unchanging
>   Rising along the line of treetops blood fusing with water   Madness   Madness
Bewitched by the sun, blinding darkness

>   Then falling   Feet first
Feet staring, on the road in all directions, hang great rocks painfully trussed
>   Light   Mole's stark white pointed teeth
In the green shade tear out the mountain's entrails
>   A cicada screams in alarm   Clamour of a terrible thrashing
Bone marrow, slimy snails, meandering through valleys
>   Self-consuming like echoes

Unless mad and pursue death, you
>   Must   Once more be abandoned   Dawn lets go and running amok charges up
The blue resounds with tearing, the sun plays with a vengeance
>   Only a snake coiled in the heart watches
Light comes from a place of winter sleep and there
>   Must   Be a heap of fire   Total nakedness   Death and ecstasy suffering yet pure

Golden kernel, graves with the power to induce deep sleep
>   In the afternoon it is one, but clusters of fruit   When thrown to the stars
In the flesh it is one, seizing and grabbing
>   Another heaven   Mute bog   Unflowing blood
Madness   Madness is god   Dead on the altar
>   Resurrected beneath the left breast a setting sun pierced in agony
Birds as they want to be: substance

"Mountain" No. 2[20], *In Symmetry With Death*

---

20 This poem is based on the legend of Kuafu pursuing the sun.

A woman in white hemp gives birth on the tattered clothing of a wall painting
    A hand clutching the earth and weeping
    A face disintegrating
    Soaked full of water
    The wind is all blood
    Dead teeth chewing grass
    Savagely extinguishing nerves afflicted with tropical fever

Soft like snow, when gauze is washed its purity flows away
No-one seduced her, her abdomen trembles
In the Third Month two orioles chase each other high up
Calling two stars
Betrayal and war   *Stony stream shallow*
                 Flying dragons soar

    From these arms to another's, she calmly presents herself
Like an ever-flowing goblet
Open swamp, repeated plummeting
She allows enemies to enjoy death on her body
Her only enemy is Death's
Small white stalk

    The woman splits open to the earth
    Squashed soul
    With each breaking of the water sac earth sinks into earth
    Ageless grave figurines
    Bodies touch   Are baked   Swallowed again and again
    All a pile of ash from menstrual flows

    Living   Living   Stone tortoise's sleepy eyes drowsy
    Vast darkness
    Utterly squandered on an empty coffin
Fearing death of her beloved in an assassination
She again beautifies herself, history of illness is her beauty
Raped, the cries of birds rising all around
At the moment of the polygamous marriage, ecstatic orgy
No wonderful traces   *Suddenly turning back tears flow*
                 Grieving there is no woman on the high mound

    Beautiful marsh of a pile of silk and brocade
    Loses its last memories
    Woman wearing white hemp

Suddenly turns into a shadow at the sound of farewell
Wall paintings at her feet cracks deepening
Like an untiring mirror

While trapped there is kissing
This vast land is planted with corpses

"Earth" No. 4 – "She: Xi Shi"[21], In Symmetry With Death

Four prose-poems which are absurd social satires form the centrepiece of *In Symmetry With Death*. The following is one of these pieces which are at the same time Orwellian, Kafkaesque and reminiscent of Lu Xun's *Wild Grass*:

One story goes: Afterwards, people all turned into cockroaches, that is those creatures that peep out of cracks in the wood of cupboards and steal in and out – but don't mock them, they are virtually the only insects to survive several ice ages, not only have they lived on but they have changed very little in form – their capability to survive is strong, and definitely mankind which appears so wonderful has nothing on them.

The Theory of Evolution is really quite amazing!

Another story goes: Later on cockroaches got sick of being burdened with legs (why rush about day and night just to exist and brave dangers for the sake of fame and glory? why risk maiming oneself by wielding weapons to fight over the opposite sex?), and one morning, they all turned into moss. From what is said, even in harsh environments like the stars, their brethren stoically exist so that now they maintain a sort of cosmic arrogance.

Don't wrongly assume that they have died: have a closer look, the whole planet is changing colour!

Finally, the good fortune of man defies all description. Although unworthy of being counted as one, it is quite beyond my ability to describe even myself. If I use the metaphor "hollowed-out rock", it still falls short of describing the tranquil, transcending, beautiful, not needing to eat and drink, neither light nor dark, neither hot nor cold – simulation of death, which is more powerful than death; it is sluggish living.

It is this which is known as the the state of "ineffability"!

---

21 Xi Shi, famous beauty of the Spring and Autumn period. She was presented by Goujian the King of Yue to Fu-chai the King of Wu as part of a political bid for peace. On the defeat of the state of Wu she was taken by the barbarian conquerors.

Let's not concern ourselves with trifling matters, this world has in fact never stopped, best to forget it – even if it rolls over our bodies, sending blood flying everywhere, it should be regarded as the natural thing, there are lots of people born without arms and legs; even if it becomes cold, unbearably cold so that even the ends of the nerves turn to ice, needless to say the valves of the heart would have long since become the poles of the perpetually frozen earth, still all one needs do is to put some effort into quickly turning into a cold-blooded animal so that it will be convenient to hibernate.

In the seasons when contagious diseases are rampant I lurch about the streets (if I don't then it's likely that I will before long be carted off by the corpse-collecting teams) and like everyone else be holding onto my head, wailing and looking beseechingly everywhere. Of course, not expecting a response. These days who doesn't think the other person has a terminal disease?

In times when writing becomes fashionable, everyone is a poet, cockroaches and rocks also take part in the civil service examinations. If I make it to high school, I'm really great – how can I be an exception? Write write write write, like an untreated disease.

In the market place of time, I am like a fish in water, encountering springs all around. In this investment there is nothing more important than patience. Anyone who can wait a hundred years will be able to sell off any little gadget for a handsome profit. If anyone can stake all and stick it out for a thousand years, then even a scrap of paper will be worth a fortune. – Hng, I've always despised little tricks like making fake antiques!

To live is to learn, to live for a long time is an art!

There will always be good butchers subsidising benevolent clubs, so that artists there can research the techniques of suicide and slaughter: those guilty of boldness will have their testicles cut out, those who are insolent and outspoken will have their windpipes cut. There will always be auctions for cardiac arrest sufferers and beauty contests for those with eczema, moreover there will always be mass audiences at deaf-mute performances.

Colour is emptiness. Emptiness is colour.

In my nuptial chamber, high and low and all around is pasted the big red character for "Double Happiness". Suddenly I see four children walk in, each of them with faces identical to my own. They bow and say to me –

"I am your son, congratulations on your marriage"

"I am your son, congratulations on your inheriting property"

"I am your son, congratulations on your success and fame"

"I am your son, congratulations on your death"

"Mountain" No. 6, *In Symmetry With Death*

In the poems of the third and fourth books of ♀ , *Living in Seclusion* and *The Descent,* Yang Lian discards the masks of historical figures and legend in his poetic discourse. He now directly confronts himself as part of a present reality which he perceives simultaneously to embrace his past. Artistically, the poems indicate a greater poetic sense of cold detachment despite the more personal nature of the concerns of the poems and the unambiguous nature of the poet's emotional intensity. Many stark images dealing with the creative process begin to emerge. These are the images he later refines to the compressed short lines of the six-line poem form which he adopts in *Masks and Crocodile.* In essence, the collections ♀ and *Masks and Crocodile* cover the same philosophical and emotional areas; the different poetic treatment employed in the latter collection concisely summarizes ♀ .

It was soon after Yang Lian had completed *In Symmetry With Death* in 1986 that he acquired a Hong Kong edition of Goya's last paintings. Goya's grotesque images of humanity were a confirmation and re-affirmation of Yang Lian's own poetic images. By the beginning of 1987 he had written the fifteen poems of *Scenery in a Room,* the last of which is "Last Room in Goya's Life" (Geya yisheng zuihou de fangjian), before starting on *Living in Seclusion* in February. The following poems selected from *Living in Seclusion, The Descent* and *Scenery in a Room* provide the final touches to this backdrop of poetry for viewing the poems of *Masks and Crocodile.*

Twin winds close this door and that door
The four seasons stack into a pile between two mirrors
A bright tunnel one can't get through
A head shoved into quicksilver
Does not breathe   Whites of my eyes not yet developed
Are daubed with four walls

Exiled to a corner of the street like a solitary public lavatory

People come and go in an obscene painting crumbling to dust
Flimsy genitals   Flattened into parallel lines of light
Stretching out yellowish claws the colour of the fur on a dead cat
Protected by my inverted reflection   I fight with myself over the
          water-marked mirror
Within this collared spout cup after cup of yellow tea
Pour in and out   Moon
Like a hacked-off thumb retches at the sound

Sweet and rancid this death has the feel of early morning
Wrinkled   Empty   Heart locked inside the door is crumpled toilet paper
Delicate wrapping of skin
Deafly spies on me   Surreptitiously disappears
Beneath thin flesh this mirror is a piece of blinded white

Staring at me
Dark abdominal cavity and twin world on the horizon
Wind and wind fleetingly brush   Face   Splits apart
Stuck like scraps of filth onto a vast stretch of quicksilver
Stomach writhes like a mountain shifting
A rib bone totally at a loss   Is seized
And scraped clean on both sides

Public lavatory forgets who has been
The loneliness is but a hazy shadow gradually moving deeper and further away

"Marsh" No. 3, *Living in Seclusion*

From now on the departing world and the departing me walk hand in hand

From now on the Valley of Death in my unmoving body
Chisels out a channel
A distant journey with the pattern of chaotic flowers strides into the sun

Striding into all this before the eyes which had once been hallucination
As if in the eyeballs   Bones are growing
Water without hardness   Shapes white stalactites
Into calcified girls
Who leap about on the grass so gracefully

As if true life is no longer hidden only after death

Behind the eyelids of unseeing eyes an expanse of real mountains and rivers
Awakened by the sad cries of a cicada on a summer night
Polished by the touch of sounds which have departed a thousand times
Turning all that are two more suddenly and longer into a unity

The more it is I   The more it is the world
Wherever each bird has fled   The Valley of Death
Stretches   In this time and place
Omnipresent   Ploughing over a blackened corpse

Radiance of the stars   A tulip experiences total realization

"Distant Journey" – "Fire" No. 8, *The Descent*

Finally   This room moves into the distance   A dog
Jumps down to the sand to drink wine   To drink from a skull soupspoon
Its only liquid

In the end floating into a scene of a multitude of people
On a dark marsh   Bushy forests slaughter the sky
Birds in agony
Lament their impotence in stirring the vast land

Bewitching maidens gather like a mass of limp flowers
Presenting lovely genitals to mountain goats
They dance in celebration   Only dead fish have once lived
Eyeballs staring blank and dazed
Crumbling

No-one understands   This huge black pomegranate head
Bloated with the ears rotted off
How the loneliness heard levels out all lives
How the years and months are houses for changing mourning clothes
In the flesh is dried-out wood   Cracking
Nailing the mute upon the wall
Arms and legs flailing   Congealing into a net
Corpses swim in single file through   Nostrils flaring in alarm

The last day follows closely after   A length of wind-dried marrow
Shaped like an arched bow
In bursts of whimpering   Goes slack   Mute silence

Now   This wall overgrown with ears
No longer hears   Tempest scattering candlelight into the distance
This pen touches blind spots spreading everywhere

Like many soundless mouths opening
Rocks swallowing loneliness
In deep places   Lair-like   The entire world is squandered
Until the room is crammed with unknown ghosts
Circling the bed in song   Eternal in the instant of impending death
– The world   When you cannot comprehend it
Listen intently

"Last Room in Goya's Life", *Scenery in a Room*
(12 December 1986)

YANG LIAN

MASKS & CROCODILE

MASKS WHICH CAN'T
BE TAKEN OFF

Did I write these poems in Australia or China?

That morning. In Sydney. A room by the sea. The sun suddenly streamed in and in the rippling light reflected from the waves, the masks covering the walls came to life and with their many layers of eyes considered me.

On so many mornings. In Beijing. My room called "Ghost House", like a fossil deeply buried in the yellow earth, drew into its embrace thousands upon thousands of years and months. So many forgotten faces had once lived but now, through the folk art tradition of carving masks for warding off evil spirits, have shrivelled into a single shadow. Unmoving laughter; brightly painted-on weeping.

Magnificent museums imprison the long history of masks in gold-plated frames. In ancient Xi'an the heavy earth has lifted a corner, allowing crushed porcelain figures to look mutely upon the living. In Tiananmen Square, drain pipes are blocked: in pile after pile of blood and flesh are the ears, noses and mouths of people.... With a greater indifference than death they look at me. In their eyes I am more of an illusion than a mask. The shadow of a shadow which died long ago at birth.

I wonder whether or not I actually wrote these poems? These words, mysterious Chinese characters, are each and every one an old house and within their four walls countless time has ebbed away. I think it was on the water, that I listened and heard the sound of someone's receding footsteps within myself. The footsteps were forever receding into the distance but never reaching anywhere. I go to say something but on the page of white paper there are the reverberating echoes of someone else. Poets have confronted poetry in this way for a thousand years.

Perhaps poetry never exists. It is only an expanse of loneliness, like the quiet loneliness of birds singing at dawn. Words are born in this way and thus have silence as their ultimate brilliance:

> The myriad phenomena is blue
> The blue of when I no longer exist

Perhaps the poet can only like a phantom perpetually wander from word to word and from mask to mask, forever in search of the other self awaiting in another time and in another place.

My face long ago was hung on a wall. These words are a wall. Totally despairing of the world, they are spoken out or else die from prolonged indecisive muttering. With every second my face becomes more wooden, turning into the face of someone else. My eyes become more and more empty, letting maggots dig a grave inside, unleashing the great slaughter which accompanies life. Lying to oneself and feigning blindness to crime become habit, to soothe and to comfort. Immersed too long in the darkness, we have already fused as one with it.

Then how is it possible for us to know? Under the filthy mask which can't be taken off, whose are those forever changing stares? Whose are the different voices muttering the same words? When names have departed, to whom do the nameless bodies belong? And when each day corpse-like falls from our bodies, who are all the empty shadows still left breathing?

Are they the numerous forgotten faces which have crossed through time and returned to my body? Or is it that my face, like these poems, after being forgotten gets to know them and quietly grows with them?

Then, everywhere is here. This instant is quite eternal.

Perhaps this room by the sea in Sydney has already waited a thousand years. The dead are all living and all shadows remain within the body: never-ending waves in motion like the sea. But my old room in Beijing, has only ever embraced one kind of time – when I can no longer recognize my own face, I recognize all other faces; when all words recede far into the distance, a line of poetry remains in my hands.

That morning, when birds were singing, it was profoundly quiet.

Yang Lian

Auckland, 9th September, 1989

1

Masks are born of faces
copy faces
but ignore faces

masks   are born on blank pages
cover the blankness
but still there is only blankness

2

This word has your face
intricately carved
woodenly polished a thousand times

finally   forgotten torn down
spread out all bloody
you hear God retching

3

Faces crumble silently
nightmares in the flesh
inch by inch chisel you away

shipwrecks
and fallen-out teeth
chatter with mud and slime

4

You stare at faces inlaid in wood
corners of eyes black and rotten
splintering

stare at faces colliding with faces
on dry cracked walls
not seeing the "you" before the mirror

5

Painted faces are like the words of lies
suddenly spat out in the moonlight
crowds of casualties sleepwalk

dead fish one after another
turn over as if born
their white   striking the darkness

6

Terrain undulating suspiciously
in dialects
the patter of birds approach

in spring it is schizophrenic talk
then silence again
green and yellow   gibberish

7

The face silent throughout
you hiding behind
telling lies

the face too is made to speak
as if also cruelly deceived
lies

8

You copy nothingness for a thousand years
on canvas indefinite smiles
ancient rubbings of faces

reproduced exactly in museums
just one page of history
long buried in the book of "you"

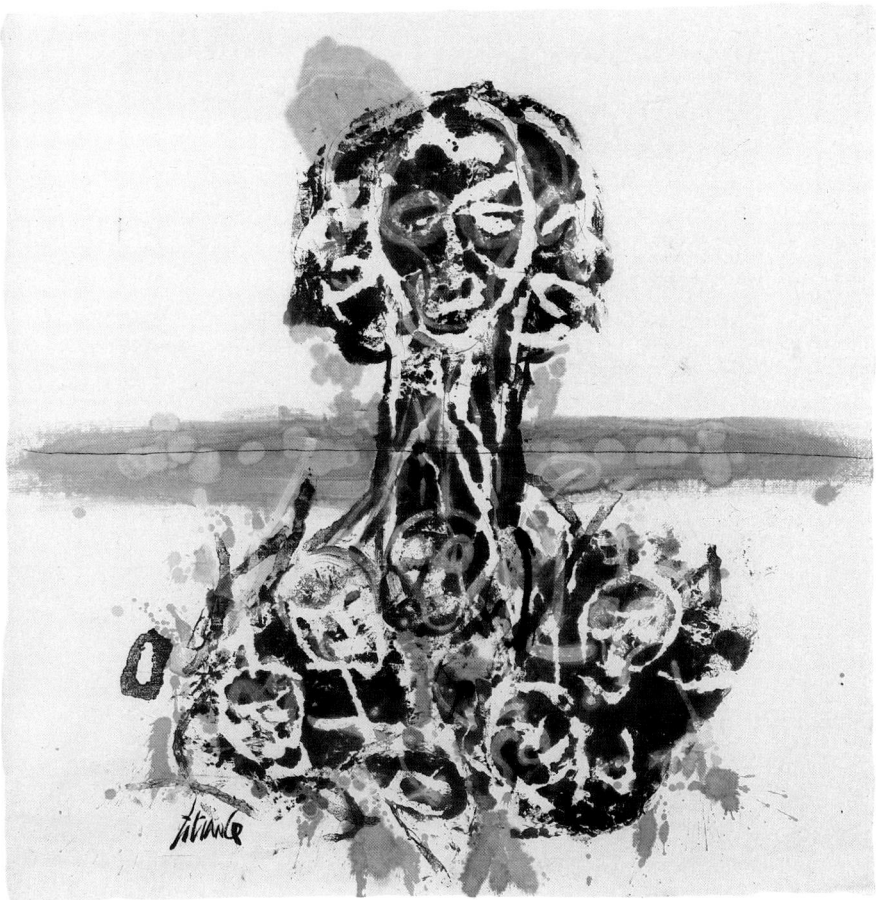

Untitled 101 x 101

49

Untitled 68 x 120

9

False faces no longer must be hidden by paint
or rouge
or black cloth

they are flaunted on streets
under superficial smiles
faces have fled far away

10

Searching for a drop of water in the sea
is like under a mask
searching for someone

you hear him speak
hear the sound of blood
and the draining of flesh

11

Birds glide on a rope path in the sky
and suddenly soar up
as if scaling a sheer precipice

one word   reads the jade heaven
balances on the wind
and is gone in an instant

12

There are many lost faces in things forgotten
piled up in layers   like mushrooms
crowding to open their mouths

the white of illness or dream
makes memory a bacteria
propagating vast forgetfulness under each face

13

You mortgage yourself to a word
to an engraver's scalpel
are carved into greater muteness than loneliness

words run amok on your lips
are flaunted on your face
squander the irredeeemable sound of laughter

14

The past silently gnaws at the wood
at dusk this face
keeps growing old

to the holes multiplying with time
each borer
returns   to eat in the darkness

15

Not within time is there peace
nor in death is there
a resting place for a face

the sea   writhes like a shrew
you stare agape at the reef
rub shoulders with it as you pass

16

You loudly address the walls
creating a wall as you speak
you are hung up on that wall

walls move everywhere
walls look at walls
walls face walls in mute silence

17

Solitary teeth scorning all
distanced from the face
from sounds spoken

the voice is eroded
everything chewed over
is more stone-like than teeth

18

The child's jawbone small but hard
plucked out by Death
learnt soundless prattle

the living on whom these milk teeth
for years have looked
are now old and wrinkled

19

You know a face
and the echoes behind it
distantly transmitted

from the White Bone Constellation
eyes avoiding you in the darkness
echoes plummeting aimlessly

20

Mirrors cannot capture faces
nor capture uneven textures of words
there is no world behind mirrors

when the face turns away
there is calm
and another face

21

The epitaph is the last mask removed
people who have discarded their faces
finally recognize one another

begin to speak the same language
when ears rot off
the sea   boring through skulls is louder
and clearer

22

The dead look upon cities from afar
eyes of marble
wrapped in the sound of birds

the sea has chosen this graveyard
for the dead to observe
marble rotting faster than faces

23

Mould stealthily grows in the morning
moist teethbeds
as in life furtively whisper

smiling at one another
Death washes your face
and features flow away like water

24

The lie kills the liar
like the face kills
the one stalking the face

and the face too is killed
abandoned on the wall by the lie
lips break into a grin like a crack

Untitled 101 x 101

Untitled 101 x 101

25

Many words parade on blankness
many unfamiliar faces
distantly collide

pile in one on the other
like an unfamiliar face
different words are at the same time blankness

26

You buried alive deep in the face
can only desperately curse
endless bad weather

corners of eyes going mouldy
the epitaph overgrown with moss
crumbles overhead beyond the corpse's reach

27

You were soft when born to words
like whitewood
with the lustre of skin

words made you brittle
everywhere
broken you are like a house full of masks

28

Someone in this sentence speaks of you
footsteps shake
the empty old house

a rusty black wind vane
paint peeling off
has waited a long time to throttle you

29

A mask never talks to itself
in silence there is murder
masks only communicate in mask-talk

in death there is eloquent language
God is a word spoken in dream
and scraped out with a mouthful of plaque

30

You look at masks in the house by the sea
as sunlight on the water floods in
under each face are countless faces

speaking together   rippling
looks drown you
flowing away you see that all creation is you

CROCODILE

1

The crocodile attacks with a glance
eyelids sheath-like
hiding sleepless teeth

flesh a mass of tiny tracks
at the water's edge
in an instant off guard you are eaten

2

Huge mouth on the other's face
you with just a set of false teeth
broken ink-green coral

fake blood   jaws open
posturing to terrify
caving in

Untitled 101 x 101

Untitled 101 x 101

Untitled 101 x 101

79

Untitled 68 x 140

3

Greasy scales in stagnant water
you feel swarms of ants
crawling from bone joints

pregnant after spasmodic itching
ovaries like an anthill
crawling with flesh-eating crocodiles

4

Ecstasy in the sound of tearing
beauty in the shrieking of skeletons
your name sharpens your teeth

your blood   shares your pleasure
in sending others to death
you again kill yourself

5

Lies attack from the marrow's slime
under layers of armour you crumble
walls collapse

fall all around
waterweeds listen
to a battle of empty bodies

6

After wild killing and feasting
comes remorse
like a fit of burping

perhaps apologies from the dead
for the host's stomach
being sour with indigestion

CROCODILE

7

The crocodile's nostrils shut like a word
ignoring you
floating and sinking on the page of white paper

despairing you call for help
and with long submerged words
sink into crocodile waters

8

Vague hatred permeates the green swamp
your days pass
wrapped in the skin of a corpse

slimy gliding
hung up   one skin is plenty
white-night-like flaunting nothingness

9

Hardened tears of many centuries
proliferate the black spots of old age
you are impeccably docile

and stare at the fish on the bank
savagely biting your nails
stupidly hiding perpetual hunger

10

Prehistoric bloated reptiles
stretch days into shadows
enough food for a whole street

coughing means dust
but a morning of copious salivating
again paints wooden smiles

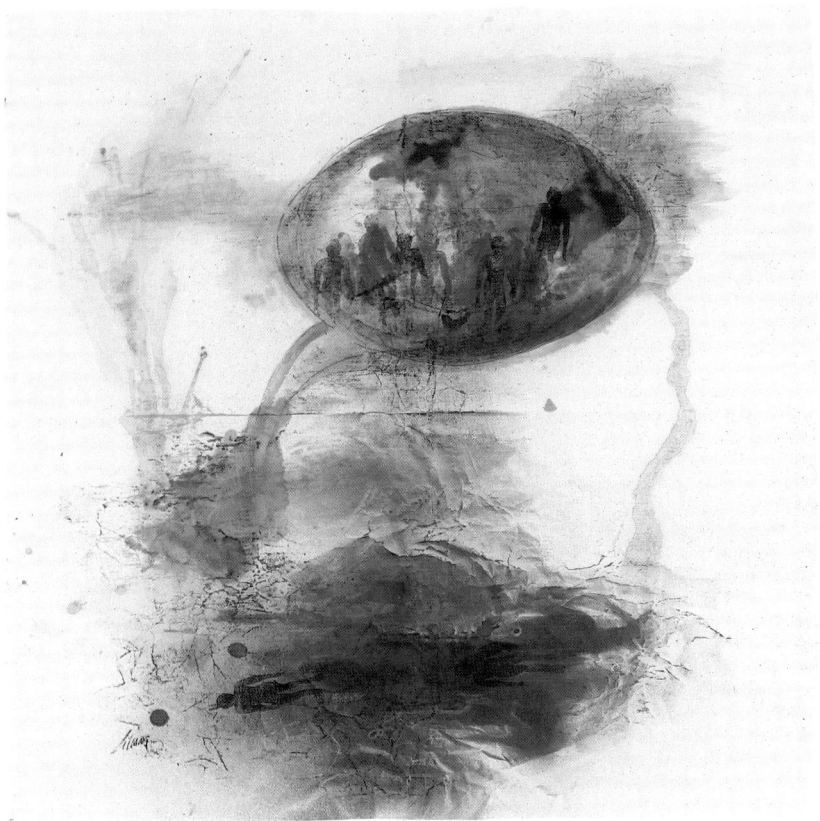

Untitled 101 x 101

Untitled 100 x 115

11

A word can take you to a dead-end
only hidden in sunlight
can there be nakedness in the absence of words

or buried in darkness' body
other moonlight under the skin
is there no need for words and clothing

12

Quiet is an impasse
the crocodile's white-hot breath looms
deceiving yourself you can endure more

deluded by a loose tooth's
faltering voice
in your silence everywhere are lies

13

Sitting alone deep at night
many crocodiles steal onto the bank
like intangible poems

crawling between fingers
under masses of grass and leaves
unknowingly you are being eaten

14

Your being is planned at conception
and as the first word grabs and kills you
your birth is induced

pale body growing with the cold
you ponder the world in a line of poetry
then comes authentic death

15

Your hand with the pen is gashed
as if seized by a crocodile
pouncing on the sun

then soundlessly dropping
the pen is seized by words
but the crocodile's belly still rages with hunger

16

One word considers you at length
more silently
than a lurking crocodile

throat soft and warm
this black tunnel
sees you deleted from the world

17

No-one drowned in this line of poetry
the deceased is only a name
and an anonymous body

so all "no bodies"
cram into this one line
sometimes surfacing to breathe

18

Unnamed persons refer to someone
maybe it is "you"
or some other "you"

but "you" remains unnamed
snapped in the jaws of a crocodile
you are terrified   "you" are all awfully cramped

19

In using a word age is forgotten
in a line of poetry there is old age at will
or youth with glib talk of death

hung up like this
sliced by the sound of the clock
and stilled by the blatant crime

20

Each word is destined to be a lie
and you rely only on a page of white paper
or the silver flowers of funerals

then   you too are nothingness
and with time together ebb away
expressing yourself again in images

21

You curse that the days abandon you
but this word erects four high walls
time too makes a lonely escape

the loneliness is surrounded by you
you hear the sound of curses
transmitted in the pervading deathly quiet

22

A paper menu envelops passing time
so you are perpetually eating
hungry thirsty words

covered in dirt
yellow calcifications on teeth
are closer than you to this moment

23

Staring at a poem
until from the blank depths a face emerges
a smile of exquisite beauty like a trap

the face absconds   a skull with gaping eyeholes
filled with wordless blue skies
when understood is ironed flat

24

The crocodile's loneliness of many colours
is magnified by a drop of water
and forged into terrifying bronze weapons

birds of the imagination are trapped
in the sky's bog
sounds of swallowing in the blue and white

25

In silence you search for sounds
captured by crocodiles or names
the mute drama of death

plays on
with the single act of curtain call
prolonged thundering applause of forgetfulness

26

The child with a mouth of crocodile-sharp teeth
slowly grows   expands
drifts up into the air

as if alive
an ugly corpse spat out by death
again licked clean by blunted existence

Untitled 101 x 101

107

Untitled 68 x 140

27

A crocodile trails everyone
shadows think other shadows are bodies
gnashing teeth swarm in

there stand
a land of shadows preoccupied with eating
shuffling dangled from the jaws of misfortune

28

You still do not exist among new names
from one word to another
you move about like a phantom

hiding in a patch of blue
the wind reads one word and the next
you do not die   you were never born

29

Words in words   persons in persons
years and months proliferate like phantoms
scraping you like a crocodile's fat belly

countless last days shift into a birthday
choked to death by a living lie
your empty shadow keeps moving away

30

The unchanging weight of death
drops into the crocodile's eyes
you calmly watch yourself swallowed up

only in blind darkness
do you hear all creation thriving on cold blood
one word sums up the world

面具与鳄鱼

摘不掉的面具

—《面具与鳄鱼》序

我不知道这些诗是写在澳大利亚还是中国？

那天早上。在悉尼。一个靠海的房间。阳光骤然亮起，粼粼水波里，满墙面具活起来，用层层叠叠的眼睛看着我。

那许多早上。在北京。我的名为"鬼府"的小屋，象一块深埋在黄土下的化石，把成千上万年的岁月拥抱在怀里。那么多被遗忘的脸，曾经活过，如今却只在农民们世代流传的、雕刻避邪脸谱的手艺里，萎缩成一个影子。一动不动地笑。大红大绿地哭叫。

高大的博物馆里，镀金画框囚禁着脸的漫长历史；古老的西安，沉重的土地掀开一角，被压碎的陶俑们，目瞪口呆地与生者面面相视；天安门广场上，下水道堵塞了，一堆堆血肉中有谁的耳朵、鼻子、嘴……它们看着我，比死亡更冷漠。我在它们眼里，比面具更虚幻。影子的影子，刚刚诞生却久已逝去。

我不知道我写了这些诗、还是没写？这些辞，神秘的中国字，每一个是一座老房子，四堵高墙内流失了数不清的时间。好象在水上，我侧耳聆听，身体里另一个人渐渐远去的脚步声。只有远去，却永无抵达。我开口说话，一页白纸上荡开不知是谁的回音。诗人和诗已这样对峙了千年。

或许诗从来是没有的。它只是一片寂静，象清晨群鸟歌唱时那么寂静。每一种语言，因此诞生，因此以沉默为终极的光明：

115

万物是蓝

当我缺席时那么蓝

　　或许诗人只能从一个辞到另一个辞，一张面具到另一张面具，象隐身人一样永恒流浪，永远寻找，那等在某时某地的另一个自己。

　　我的脸也早已被挂在墙上。这些辞就是一堵墙。世界厌倦透了脱口而出或再三沉吟的死亡。每一秒钟里，我的脸越来越麻木，变成别人的脸。我的眼睛越来越空洞，听任蛆虫在里面挖掘墓穴，展开一场与生俱来的大屠杀。温情脉脉地，习惯对自己说谎，摆出一个姿势，对触目的罪恶视而不见。太久地沉溺于黑暗，我们与黑暗已融为一体。

　　那么，我们怎么能分辨：这块摘不掉的肮脏面具下，那不断更换的眼神是谁的？嗫嚅着同一话语的不同嗓音是谁的？当名字离开，一具具匿名的躯体是谁？当每天象一个死者，从我们身旁倒下，一个个仍在呼吸的空白影子是谁？

　　是那么多被遗忘的脸，穿过时间回到我身上？还是我的脸如同这些诗，被遗忘后，结识了他们并一起悄悄生长？

　　那么，到处都是这儿。这片刻已足够永恒。

　　或许悉尼这靠海的房间，已等了千年。死者都活着，所有影子停在身体里，一直象海一样波动。而北京我那古老的小屋，从来只拥抱过一个时辰 — 当我认不出我的脸，我却认出了每一张脸；当所有辞远离，手中却留下一行诗。

　　那天早上，鸟叫时，很静。

杨炼

一九八九年九月九日于奥克兰

一

面具自脸诞生
模拟脸
又忽略脸

面具　自空白之页诞生
掩饰空白
又仅有空白

二

这个字有你的脸
精雕细刻
无表情地打磨了上千次

最后　被遗忘撕下
血淋淋摊开
你听见神呕吐的声音

三

脸无言崩溃
恶梦在肉里
一寸一寸把你凿空

海难后的船只
牙缝松驰
与烂泥混为一谈

四

你盯着那些脸嵌进木头
黝黑腐朽的眼角
木屑纷纷

盯着　脸和脸磕碰在
干裂的墙上
无视镜前的你

五

彩绘的脸犹如谎言中的字眼
一旦啐出　月光下
病人就成群梦游

一尾尾死鱼
诞生似的翻起
以空白　触摸黑暗

六

地貌可疑地起伏
在口音里
鸟类蹑足走近

春天说着癔语
再次暗转
绿与黄　含糊其辞

七

脸一直沉默
而你躲在它后面
说谎

脸也被说出
象同样惨遭欺骗的
谎言

八

你用上千年临摹这片空白
画布似笑非笑
脸的古老拓片

博物馆一样重写
历史仅仅一页
久已埋在你的书里失传

九

假面无须再被油漆遮掩
或胭脂
或黑布

沿街展览
薄施的笑容下
脸已逃之夭夭

十

在海里寻觅一滴水
就象在面具下
寻觅一个人

你听见他说话
听到血液
喝干肉体的声音

十一

鸟在空中的索道上滑行
陡然升起
像攀援一道绝壁

一个字　读遍碧空
平衡着风
稍纵即逝

十二

遗忘里有许多丢失的面孔
层层叠叠　如蘑菇
簇拥着开口

或病或梦的白
以记忆为菌种
在每张脸下繁殖许多遗忘

十三

你把自己抵押给一个辞
抵押给一把刻刀
修饰得比寂静更哑默

辞在你嘴上横行
辞炫耀你的脸
挥霍赎不回的笑声

十四

往事静静吃木头
黄昏里这张脸
依旧在衰老

日渐密集的洞穴
每一只蛀虫
回了家　晚餐在暮色时辰

十五

在时间里没有安宁
死亡里也没有
一张脸停顿的地方

海　泼妇般扭动
你眼巴巴瞪着礁石
你和它擦肩而过

十六

你大声向墙说话
你说出一堵墙
你被挂在墙上

墙到处走动
墙看着墙
墙对墙哑口无言

十七

这孤零零的牙齿目空一切
远离了脸
远离了说出口的声音

声音残缺不全
咀嚼过一切
比牙齿更像石头

十八

婴儿的腭骨细小而结实
被死亡摘下
学会无声地喋喋不休

几粒乳牙与生者
对视了多年
早已苍老得皱纹纵横

十九

你熟悉一张脸
和脸后面某种回声
深邃地传来

自白骨星座
黑暗中躲避你的瞳孔
走投无路的回声

二十

镜子抓不住脸
也抓不住凸凹不平的字
镜子背后没有世界

所以脸转过去
风平浪静
是另一张脸

二十一

墓碑是最后摘下的面具
放弃脸的人们
终于彼此认出

开始说同一种语言
耳朵烂掉时
海　洞穿头颅越响越清晰

二十二

死者从远处看城市
大理石眼睛
裹入鸟声

海择定这片墓园
让死者看见
大理石比脸更快地腐烂

127

二十三

霉菌在早晨悄悄滋长
潮湿的牙根
仍象生前窃窃私语

相视而笑
死亡给你洗脸
五官水一样流下

二十四

谎言杀害了说谎者
象脸杀死
追逐脸的人

而脸也被杀死
被谎言遗弃在墙上
咧开一道裂缝似的嘴唇

二十五

许多字在空白上展览
许多脸在素不相识中
遥远地冲撞

彼此叠入
同一张脸素不相识
不同的字同时是空白

二十六

被活埋在脸深处的你
只能拼命咀咒
不间断的坏天气

眼角发了霉
爬满青苔的墓碑
在死者摸不见的头顶坍塌

二十七

你诞生在辞里时很软
象白木头
有皮肤的光泽

辞把你变脆了
四面八方
摔碎你象满屋子面具

二十八

有人在这句话中说你
脚步声震动
这空荡荡的老房子

黑锈的风向标
油漆剥落
它等了很久才掐住你的喉咙

二十九

面具从不对自己说话
寂静中一场谋杀
面具只流通面具间的语言

在死亡中咬文嚼字
神是一句梦呓
被满口牙秽剔出去

三十

你在海边的房子里看面具
当水光泛起
每张脸下无数张脸

一齐说话　粼粼
眼波把你淹没
你流走时认出万物是你

·鳄鱼·

一

鳄鱼用目光咬你
眼皮刀鞘般
藏起睡不着的牙齿

肉里条条小径
逼近水池
你被自己侧目一瞥咬死

二

嘴在别人脸上很庞大
你只剩一口假牙
残破的墨绿色珊瑚

染着血　拉开腭骨
保持恫吓的姿势
屈服

三

死水中油腻腻的鳞片
你感到成群蚂蚁
正从骨缝间爬出

阵阵骚痒地怀了孕
子宫象一座蚁塚
孵满天生食肉的鳄鱼

四

撕裂声有一种快感
骨骼尖叫的美
你的名字磨利你的牙齿

你的血　与你分享
置他人于死地时
也再次杀害自己

五

谎言自泥泞骨髓中一击
你于重重甲胄下粉碎
断壁残垣

倒向周围
水藻在聆听
躯壳里空无一人的战争

六

凶杀之后饕餮之后
依旧会忏悔
象一连串饱嗝

或死者应有的欠意
为主胃里
消化不良的点点余腥

134

七

鳄鱼象一个字紧闭鼻孔
不屑理你
仅仅在这页白纸上浮沉

你绝望呼救
用潜伏已久的字
没入满是鳄鱼的水中

八

茫然仇恨浸满一泓绿水
你的日子裹着
死者的皮肤渡过

湿漉漉滑动
吊起　一张皮已足够
白夜似的炫耀乌有

九

许多世纪硬化的眼泪
丛生黑暗的老年斑
你温顺得无从被人挑剔

只盯住岸上的鱼
狠咬指甲
笨拙地掩饰起不停的饥饿

十

史前臃肿的爬行动物
把每天拖成影子
供一条街嚼食

咳嗽意味着灰尘
而唾液横流的早晨
又涂写出浑浊的笑容

十一

一个辞足以令你走投无路
只能隐入阳光
在无言中赤裸

或埋没于幽暗躯体
皮肤下另一片月色
无须辞和衣服

十二

寂静不可逾越
鳄鱼白热的喘息更近
你骗自己时更耐心

都迷失于一枚松动的牙齿
漂浮的声音
你的沉默中到处是谎言

十三

你孤寂独坐的深夜里
太多鳄鱼静悄悄登陆
象不可触摸的诗

在五指间爬动
密集的草叶下
你不知不觉被咀嚼过多时

十四

每次构思预谋了你的存在
而第一个字捕杀你时
你被迫诞生

苍白的躯体越冷越庞大
你用一行诗推敲世界
于是真的死去

十五

你握着笔的手皮开肉绽
象被一条鳄鱼攫住
狂暴地扑向阳光

又无声溅落
笔被字攫住
鳄鱼腹中仍只有饥饿

十六

一个字长久地沉吟你
比窥测的鳄鱼
更静谧

咽喉又软又温暖
这黑暗甬道
看着你被节节删改出世界

十七

没有人掉进这行诗淹死
死者只是一个名字
和一具匿名的躯体

于是所有无人
挤满这行诗
偶而浮出水面呼吸

十八

无人称的话里肯定有某人
或许是你
或另一个你

而你仍是无人称
被鳄鱼一口咬定
你恐怖　你们拥挤不堪

十九

用一个字忘掉年龄
在一行诗里任意衰老
年轻得侈谈死

就这么悬挂着
被钟声切开
静止于明亮的罪恶

二十

每个字注定是谎言
你仅仅依托一页白纸
依托着葬礼上的银色花朵

其后　你也空白
与时间并肩流逝
象形地重申自己

二十一

你咀咒被日子遗弃
可这个字四堵高墙
时间也在孤零零逃亡

孤零零被你围困
你听到咀咒声
从四面八方的死寂中传来

二十二

一纸单薄的食谱囊括了岁月
于是你无时不在咀嚼
这饥渴的辞

浑身泥土
牙床的黄色化石
比你更近乎此刻

二十三

凝视一首诗
直到空白深处浮现出五官
微笑精美如陷阱

脸隐退　大眼眶的骷髅
盛满无字的晴空
终于读懂时已熨得很平

二十四

鳄鱼的寂寞五颜六色
被一滴水放大
雕铸成凶险的铜器

想象飞鸟陷入
天空的沼泽
有吞咽声蓝白相间

二十五

你在沉默中搜索声音
鳄鱼或名字诱捕之后
死亡的哑剧

继续上演
谢幕的唯一动作
冗长的遗忘掌声雷动

二十六

这孩子满嘴鳄鱼的利齿
慢慢长大　　膨胀
漂浮于空气中

似乎活着
一具死亡吐出的丑陋尸首
又被迟钝的生命舔食净尽

二十七

每个人身后跟踪一条鳄鱼
影子看影子是躯体
切齿声蜂拥而入

站成
饱食终日的一地影子
被厄运咬住沉沉甩动

二十八

在新的名字里你依旧缺席
从一个辞到另一个辞
你象隐身人一样行走

隐入一片蓝
风翻阅一个辞另一个辞
你不死　只是从未诞生

· 鳄鱼 ·

二十九

话里有话　人里有人
岁月幻像丛生
磨擦你如鳄鱼肥厚的腹部

无数末日移入一个生日
呛死于一句活的谎言
你空白的影子不停走去

三十

死亡那不变的重量
落入鳄鱼的眼睛
你安祥目睹自己被吞噬

伸手不见五指
才听清万物用冷血活着
一个字已写完世界